Christmas fairy things to make and do

Rebecca Gilpin

Designed and illustrated by
Katrina Fearn, Josephine Thompson, Antonia Miller
and Non Figg

Edited by Fiona Watt

Steps illustrated by Stella Baggott
Fairies illustrated by Molly Sage and Vici Leyhane
Photographs by Howard Allman

Contents

Snowflake fairies

1. Lay a mug on a piece of white paper. Draw around it, then draw around it on some purple paper, too. Then, cut out the circles.

2. To make a snowflake for the dress, fold the white circle in half, then fold it in half twice more. Then, cut a triangle out of one side.

3. Cut out lots more triangles, all around the edges of the folded piece of paper. Make the triangles different sizes.

4. Brush household glue (PVA) over the snowflake. Sprinkle it with glitter, then let it dry. Then, glue it onto the purple circle.

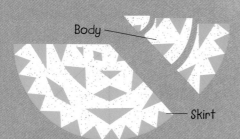

Body

Skirt

5. Cut the snowflake in half. For a skirt, cut one half into two pieces. Then, cut a shape for the body from the smaller piece.

6. Glue the skirt onto a piece of paper, then glue on the body. Cut out a purple sash and glue it on, where the pieces join.

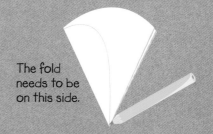

The fold needs to be on this side.

7. For the wings, draw around the mug and cut out the circle. Fold it in half three times, then draw half a wing shape, like this.

You could make a
Christmas card
with a snowflake
fairy on it.

Keep the
paper folded.

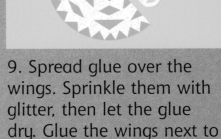

Add glittery
shoes,
too.

8. Cut along the line you
have drawn, then cut a
few triangles along the
fold, like this. Then, open
out the wings.

9. Spread glue over the
wings. Sprinkle them with
glitter, then let the glue
dry. Glue the wings next to
the body, like this.

10. Cut out a head and
some hair and glue them
together. Cut out arms, legs
and a crown and glue them
all on. Then, draw a face.

3

Glittery star chains

Cut the paper at an angle, like this.

1. To make a star, put a mug on a piece of paper and draw around it with a pencil. Then, cut out the circle you have drawn.

2. Fold the circle in half, then fold it in half three more times. Then, cut across the folded piece of paper, to make a point.

The dot shows you which point you folded first.

3. Unfold the star. Draw a pencil dot on one of the points. Then, fold the star in half from this point to the point opposite it.

4. Crease the fold, then open out the star. Fold the next point over to the point opposite it. Then, fold the others in the same way.

Press lightly, or you will squash the star.

5. To make a dip between two points, push the points together. Squash down the fold between them. Repeat this all the way around.

6. Unfold the star and gently press down on its middle, to open out the points a little. Then, make more stars for the chain.

7. Brush household glue (PVA) all over the top of a star. Sprinkle glitter over it, then leave it to dry. Then, decorate the other stars.

Use a long piece of thread.

8. Turn a star over, and put a drop of glue on two opposite points. Then, lay a piece of thread on top of the drops of wet glue.

9. Glue more stars onto the thread and leave the glue to dry. Then, cut off the bottom end of the thread and hang up the chain.

You could also decorate your stars with beads, sequins or glitter glue.

5

You could make
a sparkly star
for the top of
your tree (see
pages 30-31).

Hang the fairies
on a tree with
lots of other
decorations.

Fairy tree decorations

Use a silver pen if you have one.

1. Draw around a mug on some paper. Cut out the circle, then fold it in half. Then, unfold the circle and cut along the fold.

2. Draw two arms on one of the half-circles and cut them out. Decorate them with a pen. Then, cut out hands and glue them on.

3. For the body, decorate the second half-circle. Then, to make it into a cone, glue halfway along its straight edge.

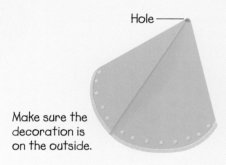
Hole

Make sure the decoration is on the outside.

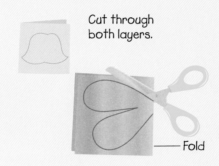
Cut through both layers.

Fold

4. Bend the paper around and press the straight edges together until they stick. Then, cut off the top of the cone, to make a tiny hole.

5. Fold two pieces of paper in half. Draw hair on one and draw a wing on the other, touching the fold. Then, cut out the shapes.

6. Draw a face and cut it out. Glue it onto one of the hair shapes. Then, cut a long piece of thread and fold it in half.

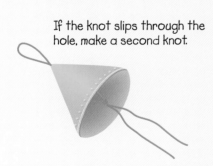
If the knot slips through the hole, make a second knot.

7. Halfway down the piece of thread, tie a knot, to make a loop. Then, push the loop through the hole in the top of the body.

8. Glue the arms onto the body. Glue the loop onto the back part of the hair, then glue the face on top. Glue on the wings.

9. For shoes, thread small beads onto the two pieces of thread hanging down. Then, tie knots below the beads to secure them.

Holly fairy collage

1. For the fairy's skirt, rip a shape from pink paper. Don't worry if it's uneven. Glue it onto a piece of paper for the background.

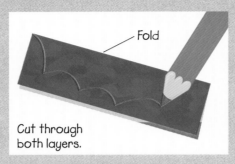

Fold

Cut through both layers.

2. For the wings, cut green pictures out of a magazine. Fold them in half and draw half a holly leaf on the fold. Then, cut out the leaves.

Join the points in the middle.

3. Unfold the leaves and flatten them. Then, glue them onto the background, just above the top of the fairy's skirt.

4. Rip a shape that is a little bigger than the skirt, from white tissue paper. Then, gather the tissue paper at the top, like this.

You could make a holly fairy and glue it to the front of a card.

5. Glue the gathered part of the white tissue paper onto the skirt. Then, cut out a body from white paper and glue it on top.

Use paper from a magazine.

6. Cut out a head, a neck and some hair. Glue the head and neck onto the hair, then draw a face. Glue the head onto the body.

Glue the feet onto some shoes.

7. Cut out arms and rip sleeves from paper. Glue them all onto the fairy. Then, cut out feet and glue them on, too.

Decorate the dress, too.

8. Cut a crown and a strip of paper for a wand and glue them onto the fairy. Add a star sequin or sticker to the end of the wand.

Spangly star wand

1. Draw a star on a piece of cardboard and cut it out. Then, put the star onto the cardboard again and draw around it.

This wand was made using bits of blue and white tissue paper.

These wands had shiny paper glued around the straw, instead of foil.

Keep the marks at the top of the stars.

2. Draw a mark at the top of the first star, then move it off the cardboard. Draw a mark at the top of the second star, then cut it out.

The slots need to be the same length.

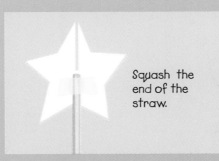

3. Keeping the marks at the top, cut a slot in each star, like this. Make the slots the same thickness as the cardboard.

4. Cut a rectangle from a roll of kitchen foil, making it a little longer and several times wider than a drinking straw.

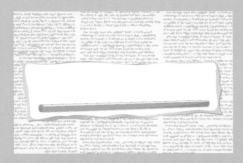

5. Lay the foil on some old newspaper and cover the non-shiny side with glue. Then, lay the straw on top, near one edge of the foil.

Squash the end of the straw.

6. Roll the straw, so that the foil sticks all the way around it. Then, tape the straw onto the star with a slot at the top.

Hold the straw in place.

7. Hold the star with the slot at the bottom, above the star with the slot at the top. Then, push the stars together, like this.

Use household glue (PVA).

8. Rip up lots of strips of tissue paper and glue them all over the stars. Cover the stars with two or three layers of tissue paper.

9. Brush the stars with glue and sprinkle them with glitter. Glue on lots of beads and sequins, or shapes cut from shiny paper.

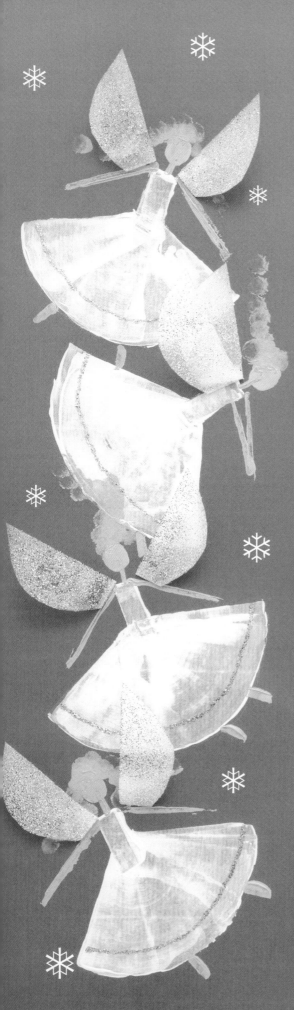

Ice fairies

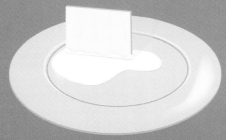

1. Pour some white paint onto an old plate. Then, cut a rectangle from thick cardboard and dip one edge into the paint.

2. To make a skirt, place the edge of the cardboard on some paper. Scrape it around, keeping the top end in the same place.

3. To make the body, dip the edge of a shorter piece of cardboard into the paint. Then, place it above the skirt and drag it across.

4. Mix some paint for the skin. Then, dip the end of another piece of cardboard into the paint. Press it onto the paper, to print arms.

5. Cut a small cardboard rectangle and print a neck and two feet. Then, dip your fingertip into the paint and print a head.

6. When the head is dry, spread a little blue paint onto the plate. Then, dip your finger into the paint and fingerprint some hair.

You could decorate the fairies' skirts with a line of glitter glue.

The part you're holding will stay sticky.

7. For the wings, sprinkle a little glitter onto some newspaper. Hold a piece of sticky tape at one end and dip it into the glitter.

8. Dip a second piece of tape into the glitter. Then, cut a corner off each piece of tape, away from the sticky end, like this.

9. Press the sticky end of the wings onto the fairy. Then, fold them back and press them down, so that the glitter is on the front.

Fairy lantern decorations

Mix the glue and water on an old plate.

1. Mix some household glue (PVA) with water, so that it is runny. Then, brush the glue all over one side of a piece of paper.

2. Sprinkle silver glitter over the wet glue, then leave the glue to dry. When it is dry, turn the paper over.

3. Mix some pink paint with a little water. Then, paint all over the piece of paper and leave the paint to dry completely.

Fold

You don't need these pieces.

4. When the paint is dry, draw little dots all over it with glitter glue. Then, draw a pencil line down the middle of the paper.

5. Draw three lines across the paper, to make eight rectangles the same size. Then, cut along all the lines you have drawn.

6. Fold one of the rectangles in half, along its length. With the fold at the top, cut a triangle off each end.

The cuts need to be at an angle.

Hold the ends together until they stick.

Tape this end, too.

7. Cut lots of slits along the folded edge of the paper, but don't cut as far as the unfolded side. Then, open out the paper shape.

8. Put a drop of glue at the top and bottom of one end of the shape. Bend the shape around until the ends meet. Press them together.

9. Tape a piece of thread inside the lantern, as a handle for hanging. Then, make more lanterns from the other rectangles.

Find out how to make this fairy tree decoration on pages 6-7.

The pink lantern below had a line of glitter glue added before it was glued together.

Glittery fairy bookmark

1. Cut a circle from paper for the fairy's head. Then, draw a shape for the hair on thick pink paper and cut it out.

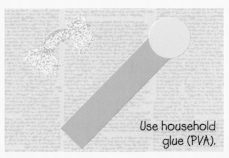

Use household glue (PVA).

2. Cover the hair with glue and sprinkle it with glitter. While the glue dries, cut a strip from the pink paper and glue the head onto it.

3. Glue the hair onto the head and draw a face. Then, cut a crown from shiny paper and glue it onto the hair.

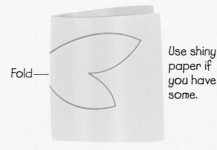

Fold —

Use shiny paper if you have some.

4. For wings, fold a piece of thick paper in half and draw a wing on it, like this. Then, keeping the paper folded, cut out the shape.

5. Glue the wings onto the back of the pink strip of paper. Then, decorate the bookmark with stickers, glitter glue and silver pens.

The snowflakes on the blue bookmark were drawn with a silver pen.

Sparkly decorations

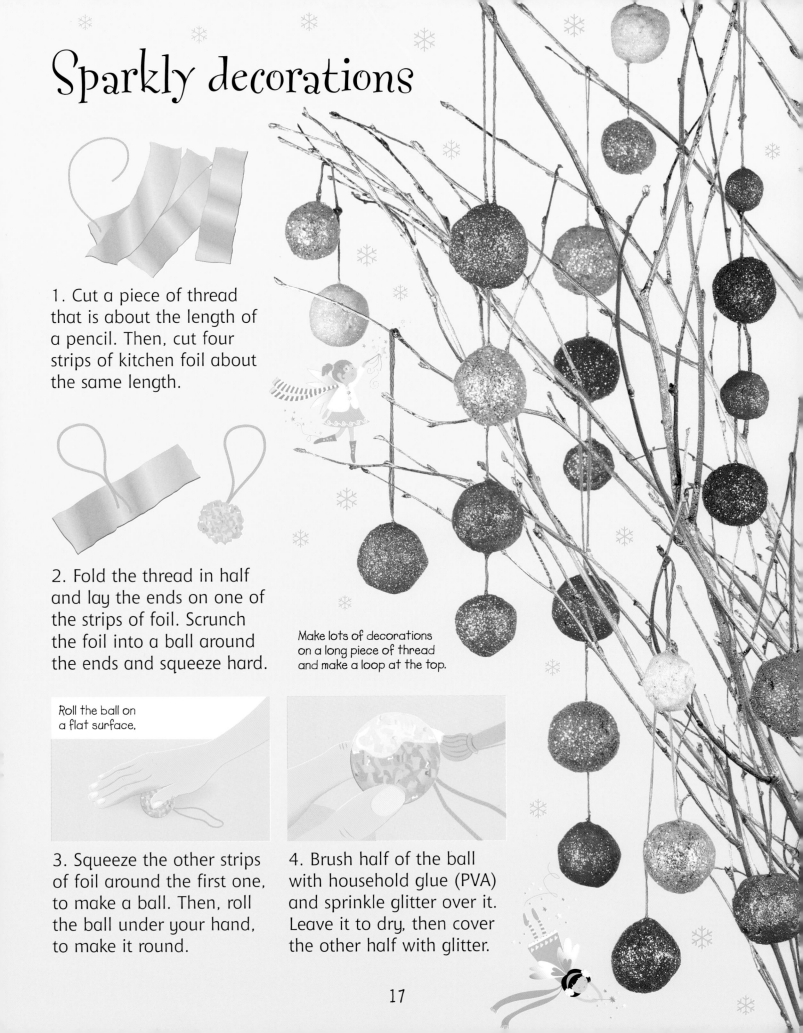

1. Cut a piece of thread that is about the length of a pencil. Then, cut four strips of kitchen foil about the same length.

2. Fold the thread in half and lay the ends on one of the strips of foil. Scrunch the foil into a ball around the ends and squeeze hard.

Make lots of decorations on a long piece of thread and make a loop at the top.

Roll the ball on a flat surface.

3. Squeeze the other strips of foil around the first one, to make a ball. Then, roll the ball under your hand, to make it round.

4. Brush half of the ball with household glue (PVA) and sprinkle glitter over it. Leave it to dry, then cover the other half with glitter.

Christmas fairy wings

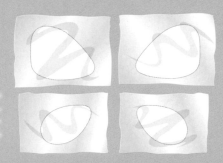

1. Draw two big wing shapes and two smaller ones on paper. Then, cut them out and lay plastic food wrap over them.

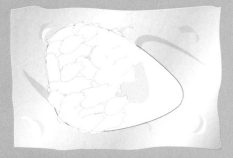

2. Rip up white tissue paper and lay the pieces overlapping on the food wrap. Cover the shapes, including their edges.

3. Mix some household glue (PVA) with water so that it is runny. Then, brush the glue over the pieces of tissue paper.

4. Rip pieces of pink tissue paper, lay them on top, then brush them with glue. Add two more layers of white tissue paper and glue.

Put the wings on your back and ask someone to tie the ribbons around your arms at the front.

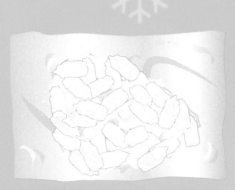

5. Sprinkle glitter over the wet glue on the wings. Let it dry, then brush another layer of glue over the top of the glitter. Leave it to dry.

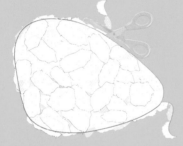

6. Peel the wings off the food wrap. Lay the paper wing shapes on top, then draw around them. Cut out the shapes you have drawn.

These wings had curves cut in the wing shapes in step 1.

7. Glue the top parts of the wings onto the bottom parts. Decorate the wings with sequins, stickers or shiny paper shapes.

Use a ballpoint pen.

8. Cut a small rectangle from thick cardboard. Make four holes in it with a pen, then thread two long pieces of ribbon through the holes.

Leave long ends on the ribbons.

9. Glue the rectangle onto the back of the wings, with the ends of the ribbons sticking out. Then, let the glue dry completely.

19

Fairy castle Advent calendar

1. To make the snowy hill, rip some white paper to make a curve. Glue the hill onto the bottom of a large piece of blue paper.

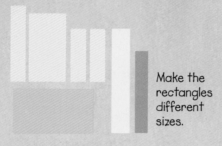

Make the rectangles different sizes.

2. For the towers, cut four rectangles from pink paper. Then, cut a large rectangle and two more towers from blue and purple paper.

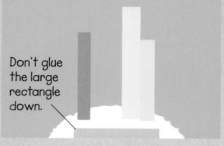

Don't glue the large rectangle down.

3. Lay the large rectangle on the hill, to show you how wide the castle will be. Then, glue the three tallest towers onto the hill.

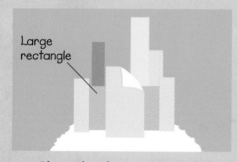

Large rectangle

4. Glue the large rectangle over the bottoms of the three tall towers. Then, glue the three remaining towers on top of the rectangle.

5. Cut out six different-sized triangles for the roofs of the towers. Then, glue one roof onto the top of each tower.

Don't make the shapes too small.

6. Cut out twenty-four doors for the calendar. Cut out some to go in the sky, flags for the roofs and windows for the castle.

Draw a flagpole with a silver pen.

7. Spread glue along one side of each door and glue it on. Then, under each one, draw a tiny picture or glue on a shiny sticker.

8. For the trees on the hill, cut out lots of green paper triangles. Then, glue them on, with some of them overlapping.

Print dots on some of the blue doors, too.

9. For snow, fingerprint white dots in the sky around the castle. When the paint is dry, write the numbers on the doors.

Tree-top fairy

1. Lay a plate on some paper and draw around it. Cut out the circle. Then, fold the circle in half and open it out.

Find out how to make these tree decorations on pages 30-31 and page 17.

Fold

2. Using a pencil, draw a line from the middle of the circle to its edge. Then, draw a wing below the line, touching the fold.

Cut here.

3. Cut up along the fold, around the wing, along the fold again and along the line. Then, cut halfway down the wing, like this.

Line up this edge and the fold.

4. Bend the wing over and gently hold it down, like this. Then, carefully draw around the edge of the wing with a pencil.

Cut here.

5. Open out the paper shape and cut around the second wing. Then, cut halfway down into the wing, like this.

6. Bend the body around so that the cuts in the wings are touching. Slot them together, then curve the body with your hands.

Draw a face.

7. Cut out a head and hair, and glue them together. Cut out arms and glue hands onto them, then glue everything onto the body.

8. Cut out legs and shoes. Draw stripes on the legs, then glue the legs onto the shoes. Then, tape the legs inside the body.

For glittery legs, like these, spread glue on the legs then sprinkle them with glitter.

9. Cut out a crown and a wand from shiny paper and glue them on. Then, decorate the fairy with stickers and sequins.

Mini fairy garland

1. Using a pencil, draw a small heart and a slightly larger one on two shades of pink paper. Then, cut them out.

2. Glue the smaller heart onto the bigger one. Then, using glitter glue, draw around the edge of the smaller heart.

Make your garland from lots of different shapes using ideas from these pages.

3. Brush household glue (PVA) all over a small piece of bright pink paper. Sprinkle glitter over the top and let the glue dry.

4. When the glue is completely dry, turn the piece of paper over. Draw a bell on the back, then cut it out.

Decorate the glittery side.

5. Cut a paper shape that will fit across the top of the bell and glue it on. Then, decorate the bell with dots of glitter glue.

24

Some of these shapes were decorated with sequins and glitter glue.

The tape stops the shapes from sliding down the ribbon.

6. Draw three stars on different shades of purple paper. Cut them out, then glue them together, with the smallest one on top.

7. To hang the shapes, cut pieces of ribbon and fold them in half. Then, tape the ribbons on, to make a loop.

8. Thread the shapes onto a long piece of ribbon and space them out. Then, tape them to the long ribbon with narrow pieces of tape.

25

Painted snow fairy card

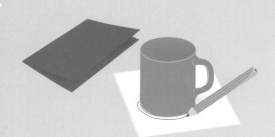

1. For the card, fold a piece of blue paper in half. Then, lay a mug on a piece of white paper. Draw around it, then cut out the circle.

2. Mix some paint for the fairy's face and body. Paint a face on the circle. Then, paint a body below it, like this.

3. Paint four shapes for the fairy's wings. Then, paint the hair and a small yellow circle for the end of the wand.

You could paint little white dots around the circle, instead of printing snowflakes.

Try painting fairies with their wands and arms in different positions.

4. When the paint is dry, outline the fairy's body, chin and wings with a black felt-tip pen. Decorate her dress, too.

5. Draw a face, then add arms, legs and lines on the fairy's hair. Then, draw a wand with a star on the end, like this.

6. Glue the circle onto the folded card. Then, paint a thin white line down from the top of the card and add a bow.

You could print a mixture of snowflakes and dots on the card.

7. To print the snowflakes, cut a small piece of thick cardboard. Dip the end of it into some white paint, then press it onto the card.

8. Print a second line across the first one and add a third line. Print lots more snowflakes around the circle.

Fairy crown

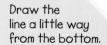

Draw the line a little way from the bottom.

1. Cut a rectangle of paper that fits around your head. This crown sits on the top of your head, so cut a little off one end.

2. Fold the rectangle in half, with the short ends together, then fold it twice more. Then, draw a line across the paper, like this.

Use hair clips to clip the crown to your hair.

Crease mark

Cut through all the layers.

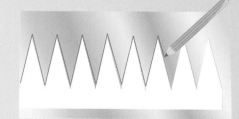

3. To mark the middle of the folded paper, fold it in half, with the long sides together. Then, press it to make a crease at the end.

4. Using a ruler, draw a line from the crease mark to each end of the line at the bottom. Then, cut along the slanting lines.

5. Unfold the paper shape, then lay it on a piece of thin cardboard. Carefully draw around the shape, and cut it out.

The cut goes halfway down.

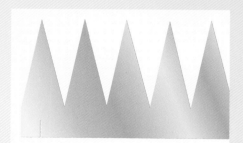

6. Cut off the triangle at one end, leaving a strip at the bottom. Then, make a cut down into the strip, like this.

7. At the other end of the crown, make a cut up into the last triangle, like this. Make the cut the same length as the first one.

8. Bend the crown around and slot the cuts into each other, with the ends inside. Then, secure the ends with a piece of tape.

Glue little beads onto
the ends of the points.

9. Bend each point out
with your fingers, like this.
Then, glue beads and
sequins onto the crown, or
decorate it with glitter glue.

Sparkly hanging hearts

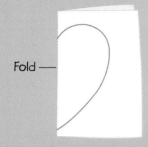

1. Fold a piece of thin cardboard in half. Draw half a heart on it, like this. Keeping the cardboard folded, cut out the shape.

2. Lay the cardboard heart on some thick paper. Draw around it four times. Then, cut out all the hearts you have drawn.

3. Fold each heart in half, from top to bottom. Then, open them out. Paint one side of one of the hearts with household glue (PVA).

4. Sprinkle glitter over the glue and leave it to dry. Then, do the same to the remaining three hearts and let the glue dry.

5. When the glue is dry, fold the hearts so that the glitter is on the inside. Then, spread glue on one half of one of the hearts.

6. Press one half of another heart onto the glue, matching the curved edge and the fold, like this. Hold it until it sticks.

7. Spread glue on the other half of the heart and press on another heart. Then, make a loop in a piece of thread and tape it inside.

8. Spread glue on both halves of the last heart and press it on, over the thread. While the glue dries, make more heart decorations.

Make lots of different-shaped decorations (see 'Other ideas' opposite).

30

Other ideas

Make snowflakes, circles and stars by drawing other shapes on the folded cardboard.

This shape makes a circle with a hole in the middle.

This will be a snowflake.

This shape makes a star.

Pretty boxes

1. Rip some tissue paper into pieces. Brush the pieces with household glue (PVA) and press them all over a box and its lid.

2. Brush glue all over the top and the sides of the lid. Then, sprinkle glitter all over the lid and leave it to dry.

3. When the glue is dry, glue sequins around the edge of the lid. Then, glue sequins in the middle too. Leave the glue to dry.

You could use any small box, such as a gift box.

Photographic manipulation: Mike Olley